VERONICA
ROTH

VERONICA ROTH

HEATHER MOORE NIVER

ROSEN
PUBLISHING®

New York

Published in 2015 by The Rosen Publishing Group, Inc.
29 East 21st Street, New York, NY 10010

Library of Congress Cataloging-in-Publication Data

Niver, Heather Moore.
Veronica Roth/Heather Moore Niver.—First edition.
    pages cm.—(All About the Author)
Includes bibliographical references and index.
ISBN 978-1-4777-7906-4 (library bound)
1. Roth, Veronica—Juvenile literature. 2. Authors, American—21st century—
Biography—Juvenile literature. 3. Young adult fiction—Authorship—Juvenile literature.
I. Title.
PS3618.O8633Z77 2015
813'.6—dc23
[B]

2014012318

Manufactured in China

CONTENTS

Once upon a time, in a land not so far away, creative writing student Veronica Roth started writing a novel. But this young writer's story did not have its origins in a writing workshop in college. Instead, she wrote furiously in fits and spurts before, between, and after classes, beginning to form her own writing habits and techniques while always striving to find the best way to tell her story.

The story of how Veronica Roth became an author is arguably just as riveting as the stories she has told as an author, namely the *Divergent* trilogy: *Divergent*, *Insurgent*, and *Allegiant*. As a student,

Little did Veronica Roth know that the novel she furtively wrote between classes at college would one day become the *New York Times* best-selling YA novel *Divergent*.

Roth started writing—and scrapped, then restarted several times—what would eventually become a *New York Times* best-selling young adult (YA) series about Beatrice (Tris) Prior. Before she graduated from college, she had a book deal—which she celebrated by jumping into a bathtub full of mini marshmallows, and then posted the video of her sweet and sticky adventure on her blog. Before she had completed the final book of her series, a film based on the first book was in the works. She also has published four short stories that provide backstory, new information, and key scenes as told from the viewpoint of Four (Tobias Eaton), Tris's mentor and love interest. That's quite a list of accomplishments for an author who is only in her twenties.

Roth is a young writer who admits she is always working to become better by learning from reviews, practice, and other experience. But she's not shy about her love for writing young adult fiction. During her time at Northwestern University, she worried about how her fondness for writing and reading young adult literature would look to others. Her creative writing professors and fellow writing students seemed to dismiss anyone who wrote fantasy or young adult fiction. They talked about it as though it were easy and not "real writing." She felt ashamed of her writing and reading tastes and hid them. She started writing *Divergent* on the side, waking up early to write before classes and continuing to write in between classes. Sometimes she was so into it that she would write instead of doing her homework. She even worked on it at the same time as she was writing her senior thesis. She just could not stop writing.

Now in her mid-twenties, Roth is a *New York Times* best-selling author whose first book was made into a film. Movies of the next two books are in the works, with Oscar-winning screenwriter Akiva Goldsman on board to write the screenplay for *Insurgent*. (Goldsman won an Oscar for his writing on the movie *A Beautiful Mind*.) It seems as though even Roth's professors and peers, who earlier had dismissed her YA reading and writing preferences, would agree that she was smart to stick to her guns and follow her heart.

ONE AUTHOR'S LIFE

The first chapter of Veronica Roth's story begins in New York State, where she was born on August 19, 1988. From there, her father's job took the family to Hong Kong and Germany, but finally the family settled back in the United States in Barrington, Illinois. Veronica's mother, Barbara Ross, is a painter who trained at the Art Institute of Chicago and mainly works in watercolor. She still lives in Barrington. Veronica's parents divorced when she was only five years old, but Veronica and her stepfather, Frank Ross, became quite close. Ross does financial consultation for landscaping companies. Veronica's two older siblings live near Chicago; Ingrid is in marketing, and Karl is a musician.

Veronica was the kid who spent all her free time scribbling with a pen and paper when she was growing up. Her mother told Christopher Borrelli of the *Chicago Tribune*, "She was a smart, serious child, introspective." As soon as Veronica got too old to play "pretend" out in the back yard, she simply transferred those imaginative scenarios to the page and started writing. After she devoured the *Animorphs* series by K.A. Applegate and Orson Scott Card's *Ender's Game*, there was no question about what she wanted to write. Veronica was hooked on young adult fiction.

WORD GIRL

As she got older, she became a studious kid at Barrington High School. It wasn't easy. She told Borrelli, "In high school, I was grouchy, defensive, and judgmental—you know how you can judge people quickly, so they don't get the opportunity to judge you first? That was me in a nutshell."

Teenage Veronica put a lot of pressure on herself to walk the "moral high ground," but eventually, after finding that it made her judgmental and stressed out, she thought better of it. She realized that striving for perfection was actually a little foolish.

Veronica did not let facing certain social challenges define her in high school. In a 2013 interview with Burt Constable of the *Daily Herald*, a suburban

ANIMORPHS

No one knows who they are.

The Visitor

K. A. Applegate

SCHOLASTIC

Roth loved reading the *Animorphs* adventures by K. A. Applegate over and over. She named the male protagonist in her own *Divergent* series Tobias after her favorite Animorph.

Chicago newspaper, her junior-year AP English teacher, June Kramer, recalled that Veronica was a smart girl who had friends, dressed well, and was involved in school activities. For instance, she sang second alto in the school choir and was in a female barbershop quartet—even though she couldn't read music and didn't think of herself as a very good singer. Veronica took voice lessons for four years so she could improve her singing.

Kramer also remembered Veronica as "a voracious reader, a very perceptive reader." Veronica did well in Kramer's class, which had an "interrelated arts" component. Students were taught how to think and write through a combination of literature, music appreciation, art history, architecture, and field trips into the city of Chicago. Veronica won the National Council of Teachers of English Award in Writing the year she graduated.

"She was fabulous," says Kramer of Veronica's abilities as a writer. "I put a lot in her college recommendation about her writing, how mature it was. It was like reading a colleague's [work]. But she worked very hard at it."

ROTH'S RELIGIOUS REBELLION

Veronica's parents were not religious, so they were surprised and alarmed when Veronica expressed an interest in Christianity in high school. Her mother's parents, who had survived the concentration camps in Poland during World War II, were religious and stressed faith to their children and grandchildren. Despite that, Veronica's mother was not religious. She was concerned at first when Veronica's high school boyfriend took her to a Christian Bible study, but when she saw her daughter's dedication to her faith, she respected her daughter's choices.

Soon Veronica's faith carried over into her fiction. During college, she was required to write a long piece as an honors thesis, so she wrote a novella based on the apostle Paul's story. In her novella, a young woman is trying to find the mother who abandoned her when she encounters a Christian heavy metal rock festival.

As with any type of literature or art, there are many different interpretations of Veronica's books. Some people believe that they are a commentary about cliques in high school or standardized testing. Others consider them to be religious allegories. Although she considers herself a devout Christian (and even though her honors thesis had a religious flavor), Veronica balks at suggestions that she's filled her novels with secret religious propaganda. "People assume there's some weird indoctrination thing hidden in these books," she told Borrelli, "because the assumption is if you're Christian, you're preachy. But that would be a horrible thing to do to kids."

While Veronica does not consider her writing to have an overtly Christian message, she is aware that her own mindfulness of the importance of religious questions seeps into the text. She admits that any deeper meaning beyond the basic plot of her books could be considered a "personal critique." She tries to keep her main character, Tris, asking questions, but she wants to steer clear of sending a religious message through her work.

Veronica is a practicing Christian to this day. Although the topic may not be an outright theme in her books, Christianity continues to be central to her personal life. Throughout the writing process and her rapid rise to fame, Veronica has faced various challenges, which she believes her faith has helped her overcome. She told James Kidd of *The Sydney Morning Herald*, "My religious beliefs have been a great help." She thanks God in the acknowledgements in all three of her novels.

OFF TO COLLEGE

Veronica applied for early acceptance at Carleton College in Minnesota. By December of her senior year in high school, she had been accepted, so she says she really didn't have to stress out about applying to any other schools. Later, she decided Carleton was not a good fit to study writing. She applied to Northwestern University and the University of Chicago and ended up attending and graduating from Northwestern's creative writing program.

During her time at Northwestern, she was in a year-long fiction class that she has described as really shaping her writing. There were fewer than twenty students in the class, and they had to critique one another's work. She told the Goodreads website, "There is nothing quite like hearing 15 smart, thoughtful reactions to your work at once. It hurt a lot, actually, but it made me and my writing so much stronger."

Critiques by her classmates eventually helped Veronica learn how to see the problems in her writing and also encouraged her to keep working on her stories. She started learning from the reviews rather than letting them

In a fiction workshop at Northwestern Univesity, Roth learned how to make the most out of peer critiques and use them to make her writing stronger.

discourage her, something she has said she continues to work on to this day.

UNLIKELY INSPIRATION

Although she was immersed in writing workshops, that's not where Veronica's identity as a writer originated. One day, as she was driving to Carleton College, she saw a billboard showing someone leaping off a building. As she continued on her long drive to school, she started to wonder why someone would do that. What would drive someone to jump off a building?

In an introductory psychology course she was taking at the time, students were studying exposure therapy. This involves having people confront their biggest fears through repeated real-life experience. Veronica latched on to this theory and started wondering what would happen if exposure therapy were used on otherwise emotionally healthy people to decrease their normal fear responses and make them braver. As she thought about it, she decided that an entire culture could develop like that on its own. Thus, she created the world in which *Divergent* is set. The world that Roth created was also inspired by the armies in Orson Scott Card's *Ender's Game*, as well as J.K. Rowling's *Harry Potter* series, in which students are divided into houses based on their personalities.

WINGING IT TO SUCCESS

In several interviews, Veronica has claimed she did not do much planning while writing *Divergent*. As she told Serena Chase of the *USA Today* website, "I'm definitely what we call a 'pantser,' which means, 'write by the seat of your pants'—so I don't outline." She just started writing and let the story develop organically.

For her second book, *Insurgent*, it was a slightly different story. When dealing with a series of books, publishers like to see a plan in place for subsequent books. Therefore, Veronica had to outline *Insurgent* more carefully. For the second book, she "sort of built on what had happened in the first book and let everything come."

PUBLISHING FASTER THAN THE SPEED OF LIGHT

Veronica's publishing story reads more like fantasy than nonfiction. She started working on a story while she was a freshman at Carleton College in Minnesota, but she didn't like where it was going and put it aside. During her sophomore year, now at Northwestern University, she started working on the story again in earnest. During her 2010 winter break, Veronica spent ten hours a day writing, for forty days straight. She told *Chicago Tribune* reporter Borrelli that she wrote "until my fingers were sore and I couldn't sleep." *Divergent* was in progress.

During her senior year at Northwestern, Veronica realized it was time to make some decisions. Due to her interest in theology and the scholarly study of religious issues, she started applying to graduate schools for a master's degree in biblical studies. She was asking herself the usual graduate-school questions—How will I pay for tuition? Where will I live?—when she was hit by inspiration. At a writers' conference in Indiana, she realized that she had copies of *Divergent* with her, as well as a pitch letter ready to give prospective literary agents and publishing houses. She approached Joanna Stampfel-Volpe, an agent at Nancy Coffey Literary & Media Representation, at the conference, giving her the pitch and a copy of the manuscript. Stampfel-Volpe read the book and proclaimed it "unputdownable." She practically signed Veronica as a client on the spot.

In an unusual turn of events, Roth got a book contract before graduating from college. On a whim, she handed her *Divergent* manuscript to an agent. The rest is history.

After some revision work was completed, the book was shopped around, meaning shared and promoted, as part of a trilogy. Before Veronica knew it, several publishers, including HarperCollins, were vying for the rights to the

NOT TAKING NO (OR THIRTY-FIVE OF THEM) FOR AN ANSWER

Before Veronica got literary representation by an agent, she had been going to writers' conferences and sending queries about her writing to agents (without mentioning her age), beginning in her junior year of college. "I'm kind of stunned by the unintentional arrogance of writing something and thinking, 'OK, I'll go try to get it published,'" she told Janet Potter of the *Chicago Reader* website. "It just didn't occur to me that maybe it wasn't good enough."

Of the thirty-five queries she had sent to agents, she only got one positive response. That lone agent declined her book in the end but asked her to send something else. With this encouragement, Veronica started *Divergent* and eventually sent it to more agents.

Divergent series. By April, the book was sold to Katherine Tegen Books, a HarperCollins imprint.

On her blog, Veronica had vowed that once she got her first publishing deal, she would fill a swimming pool with marshmallows and dive in. Realizing that filling a pool was impractical, she compromised, filling her bathtub with mini marshmallows instead. In place of the traditional rubber ducky, she placed marshmallow Peeps in the tub. She shot a video of herself (and her new agent) celebrating in the marshmallows and posted it on her blog to share the good news.

Even with two best-selling YA novels under her belt, Veronica Roth was still nervous when it came time for *Allegiant*, the third novel in the series, to hit the shelves.

IMPENDING AWESOME

One might think that by the time

the third book of the *Divergent* trilogy was published, Veronica would be used to the routine, the anticipation, and the expectations. But as *Allegiant* was about to hit store shelves late in 2013, she definitely felt some trepidation. Expectations were high, and she worried about disappointing the books' fans. As she told *Chicago Tribune* reporter Borrelli, "I have this feeling of impending doom. Or is it—impending awesome?"

A DAY AT THE DESK WITH VERONICA

A typical working day with Veronica Roth has a basic pattern. In an interview with Goodreads, she spells it out:

> Wake up. Blink a lot. Eat breakfast. Drink tea. Attempt to start writing. Get distracted. Take a shower. Get dressed. Attempt to start writing. Get distracted. Eat lunch. Attempt to start writing. Actually start writing! Write until 5. Get exhausted. Stop writing. Hang out with the three-dimensional people.

Roth doesn't work at a big wooden desk covered with papers, pens, and books, nor does she curl up all cozily on

Don't picture Roth writing at a big wooden desk covered with pens and papers. Instead, she prefers a treadmill desk so she can walk while she works.

the couch with her laptop. She writes at a treadmill desk. She doesn't like sitting all day to write, so she walks as she writes instead.

Like any writer, she experiences writer's block, but she has some tricks for getting the creativity flowing again. Sometimes she does something as simple as rewriting a section she feels isn't right. Other times she completely demolishes it and starts something new. But some days, those tricks don't work, and she realizes it's time to step away from her work completely for a while. Sometimes she heads outside for some fresh air or goes to a museum. Other times she watches movies or gets more social and talks to people.

PULLING AWAY FROM PERFECTION

One of Roth's writing techniques actually stems from a lesson she learned from her vocal coach in high school. Because she was a tense singer who needed to loosen up, her teacher told her to sing her scales as loudly as possible, no matter how awful they sounded. She admits she was terrible at this exercise, but she also found that when she went on to sing something else, she was a little bit looser and sang a little bit better.

These days, she uses this as a writing technique. When she writes her first draft, she tries to write it like no one will read it. The trick is not always successful. On her blog, she commented, "I wrote *Divergent* with all the wild freedom of someone who believes that their writing will never be seen by anyone. I wrote *Insurgent* with all the neurotic controllingness of someone who is aware that their writing will be seen by people—a lot of people."

In general, she admits to having a hard time letting her writing be totally crummy. She wants to make that first draft as good as possible. Unfortunately, her attempts to edit during the first draft actually made things worse. Roth has to remind herself to let her work be as loud, lousy, and out of tune as it needs to be at first, and remember that she can go back and revise, edit, and even completely rewrite it later.

A writer who inspires Roth is Anne LaMotte. On her blog, Roth quotes a favorite piece of writing advice from LaMotte's writing book, *Bird by Bird*. The quote talks about how perfectionism is the enemy and will make a person crazy. It is a mindset that keeps writers from producing their best work. Better that they should simply write with abandon and enjoy the process more, because the writing is going to be what it is going to be. This technique applies to any

Writer Anne LaMotte has inspired Roth and many other artists with her own creative tips, such as forgetting about being perfect. Have fun and revel in the creativity.

creative endeavor, whether it's writing or painting or music. Pulling away from perfection allows Roth to write freely, have fun, and get lost in her work.

ROTH'S REVISIONS

In an interview with Christina Radish of the Collider website, Roth explained that her favorite part of the writing process is revision. "My rough drafts are just an insane word-vomit mess. They're gross, awful and just terrible," she said. But once that first draft is done, she gets to her favorite part: getting good notes, tearing the first draft apart, and putting it all back together to finally get to the story she was trying to tell in the first place. More than that, she loves editing in the later stage of revisions when she fixes really little things and finally feels like she's seeing the finished piece.

When Roth wrote *Divergent*, she wrote so many drafts that she lost count. Her best guess is that she wrote seven or more, depending on how one defines a new draft. If she makes major changes to a work, Roth considers it a new version. She wrote two drafts before she got an agent and then three more after she signed with a publisher. Her second book, *Insurgent*, didn't require as many rewrites, in part because she was short on time to meet deadlines.

NAILING THE PERSPECTIVE

When Roth started writing *Divergent*, she wrote from the point of view of the character Four (later also known as Tobias). But something didn't seem quite right; it felt predictable and dull. So, thirty pages into the story, she put the whole book aside and started experimenting with telling the story with a new voice.

She tried out the voices of a number of characters, including Tris's brother, Caleb, and her mother, Natalie. She did some drafts using Natalie's journal entries here and there throughout the story, but she found she couldn't tackle some crucial aspects of the story even with a forward-moving narrative and the diary entries. The author was back to square one.

Four years later, Roth picked up the manuscript again and decided to switch gears, eventually writing from the viewpoint of a strong, determined female character: Tris. Roth thought it might be a more compelling story if she swapped up the gender roles. Her female character was born into surroundings where she was urged to be altruistic, or self-sacrificing—a situation Roth feels many women are in—but she struck out and acted in ways considered to be "dangerous and bold and crazy," Roth told Robin Young of WBUR radio. That kind of

In the film version of *Divergent*, Shailene Woodley *(right)* plays the main character, Tris. Roth thought Tris would be far more compelling as a strong but imperfect protagonist.

character was of more significance to Roth as a writer and made the story more interesting.

Yet Roth didn't make Tris a perfect character, because she felt the protagonist would then be boring. Instead, she purposely created a character who was difficult to like sometimes, which she told Erin Fry on the *Publishers Weekly* website was a "weird sacrifice that's always for the greater good. The stronger a character is, the more flawed she has to be."

LIKE CHARACTER, LIKE AUTHOR?

Roth is very clear that her characters are not reflections of herself. She is often asked about parallels with her heroine, Tris, and she explains that growing up she was a good teen who

ROTH'S WRITING RECOMMENDATIONS

Roth's main writing advice is to write all the time and keep at it. Even the little pieces of writing that seem like nothing can lead to something later on. Write a lot—as much as possible—and write about what interests you, she says. Always want to write more than you want to get published. She suggests getting good people to critique your work, making sure you can trust them. Never shy away from trying big changes.

On her Tumblr page, The Art of Not Writing, she tells young writers that they should:

> ... never worry about getting enough "done." All I did from ages 11–20 was write little broken pieces of stories that fizzled out after ten pages, twenty pages, fifty pages, three hundred pages...and then one day I found something that I thought was worth writing to the end. And after that I was able to finish things more often. But no time spent writing little pieces is ever wasted—*Divergent* was one of those pieces, for me, something I started and abandoned quickly after my freshman year of college and then picked up again four years later with a fresh perspective.

> Don't get caught up in worrying whether the writing is "good enough." That can smother the writing completely. Just do the best you can at the time. No writing is really wasted. Every bit of writing is just another step toward better writing.

met her curfews and didn't break the rules. And then there is the fact that Tris is a tiny blonde and Roth is a (nearly) six-foot-tall redhead.

Nevertheless, Roth and Tris do share some similarities. Roth started writing Tris's character when she was dealing with her own anxieties. When she felt held back by her life, Roth acted out brazenly. She cut her hair very short, married early, and moved clear to Romania, all toward one goal: "Like Tris, I am trying to be a richer, fuller version of myself," she told *Chicago Tribune* reporter Christopher Borrelli.

In the novels, Tris breaks out of her mold and joins the Dauntless faction—a group of daring, fearless, even reckless citizens in the *Divergent* world. Roth told *Sydney Morning Herald* writer James Kidd that writing the character of Tris was "like diving into my psyche. Tris actually grows up in an oppressive environment and chooses this bold path. I think anxiety makes your internal environment very oppressive. It makes you unable to do things you want to. Following her through this really bold move was helpful for me."

THE GOOD, THE BAD, AND THE ANXIOUS

Tris does some daring things, which is what her creator has said she is always trying to do. In fact, the year after her second book, *Insurgent*, came out, Roth underwent exposure therapy, which treats the anxiety-disorder patient by having her face her fears. The simple act of going online had become incredibly stressful, as she was facing one-star reviews on book sites like Amazon and nasty messages from readers accusing her of writing like a school kid. Treatment has helped her learn how to deal with such people and go on with her writing.

But it's not only naysayers who can be an issue. Roth also has to deal with the polar

opposite in passionately enthusiastic fans who
burst into tears when they meet her or follow
her around in hopes of getting an autograph. At

Roth's fans are so passionate about her novels that they will stand in line for hours
for a chance to meet her and get an autograph.

author signings and book festivals, Roth is faced with the task of signing books for more than a thousand fans. She's anxious that some of them wait for an opportunity for hours, and she hates to disappoint them. She wants them to feel as if meeting her was worth the wait. To ease this stress on the anxious author, her book tour for *Allegiant*, the final volume in her trilogy, only stopped in four cities.

THE *DIVERGENT* DYSTOPIA

Veronica Roth set her *Divergent* series in a dystopian world, where life is hard and nearly everything is fraught with danger. Roth and a number of her contemporaries, such as *Hunger Games* series author Suzanne Collins, are drawn to the dark, crumbling worlds found in dystopian fiction. If the fan base for these books is any indication, so, apparently, are readers of all ages.

WHAT IS DYSTOPIAN FICTION?

Utopian and dystopian literature both explore political and social structures.

CHAPTER

THREE

The *Divergent* trilogy can be filed under the ever-popular category of "dystopian fiction." The books are set in a dark, dangerous world, as shown here in an image from the *Divergent* movie.

Utopian fiction, such as Ursula K. Le Guin's novel *The Dispossessed* (1974), is set in an ideal world, or a utopia. Dystopian fiction is the opposite: set in a dangerous, hopeless world of the future, known as a dystopia. The word "dystopia" comes from the ancient Greek: "dys-" means bad, and "-topia" refers to a place to live.

Some stories include both a dystopia and a utopia to depict the contrasting choices people can make and the two futures they can end up with. The science fiction genre often features utopias and dystopias, as does speculative fiction. In fact, some argue that utopias and dystopias are a type of speculative fiction.

A DESIRE FOR DYSTOPIA

Roth has been intrigued by the genre of dystopian fiction ever since she read Lois Lowry's *The Giver*, the story of a young boy who uncovers the ugly truth about his supposedly perfect world. She soon followed that up by reading *1984* by George Orwell and then Aldous Huxley's *Brave New World*. But as much as she enjoys reading about these dismal worlds, she did not set out to write a dystopian novel herself. "When I was writing *Divergent*, I didn't know it was a thing," she said in a Goodreads interview. "I just had this story and this world and this character, and as luck would have it, it hit the market at the right time."

In fact, if the newest popular fiction was utopian in nature, Roth says she wouldn't even crack it open because it lacks conflict. Her thinking is, who wants to read about a world where everything is perfect and turns out right? Roth would be bored.

However, she has a definite vision in mind if she were to write a utopian story. In her e-book, *The World of Divergent: Path to Allegiant*, she wrote:

... if I were going to create a utopia, I would make a world in which people are focused on their personal, moral obligations, and strive to be the best possible version of themselves.

Aldous Huxley's dystopian novel *Brave New World* was one of the first books to capture Roth's attention and set her on the path to write her own such fiction.

They would be allowed to choose whatever path they wanted in life. They would know what was expected of them, they would have a clear purpose, and they would have a strong sense of group identity and belonging. And there would be five factions. . . . Oh, wait. I tried that already.

She goes on to explain that in a way, *Divergent* is her utopia. Although that's not what she set out to create, it turned out that way. She started out by writing about a place that interested her and a character who had a good story. As she wrote, Roth realized she was creating a kind of utopia…and it was awful! At first, she was sad her utopia was so crazy, but then she thought that the issue was that she wasn't sure what a "perfect" society was. "To me it's all about virtue and responsibility," she wrote in *The World of Divergent*, "to someone else it would be about happiness and peace, and happy drugs would be pumped into the water supply—but that sounds like a nightmare, doesn't it?"

Instead of despairing over this quandary, Roth embraces her inability to define perfect. She is able to stop worrying about being perfect and instead enjoy what she's doing and the people around her. In a lot of ways, she says, this is true of Tris, who first tries to be selfless, then brave, but in the end accepts that her actions are inspired by love, which turns out to be the most important thing of all.

Does that sound like a dystopia? As Roth wrote in *The World of Divergent*, "So maybe I've changed my mind—maybe I would read utopian fiction. Or maybe I already am. What a scary thought."

TENACITY FOR TEEN WRITING

Although Roth really loved reading and writing young adult fiction, she felt as if she constantly had to hide that part of her personality. Other people started telling her that the young adult fiction she was reading wasn't good enough for her—that she was too smart for it and should be reading other literature. During college, in order to keep that part of her under wraps, she found it easier to create another identity, "Classroom Veronica," who read all the right literary books. Roth told Goodreads:

> Classroom Veronica wasn't pretentious or obnoxious or anything, but when asked what her favorite books were, she didn't respond with complete honesty; she listed some adult literary fiction. Classroom Veronica can carry on an intelligent conversation about Anton Chekhov, Flannery O'Connor, Raymond Carver, and Ernest Hemingway, if she has to. If she has to, she can talk about literary fiction until it starts to come out of her ears.

Later, Roth came to see the wisdom in Eleanor Roosevelt's quote, "No one can make you feel inferior without your consent." She wished that she had stood up for the writing that was her true passion in college, even though academia wouldn't support her. She wishes she had stood up for her work and the genre and never let anyone dismiss her writing as trivial.

As she grew older, and after a solid education in literature and writing, one might expect that Roth might have grown out of her affection for the YA genre and want to write for her adult peers. Instead, she has continued to embrace her teenaged readers all the more. When asked if she was ever tempted to follow in the footsteps of YA author J.K. Rowling and try her

Veronica Roth defies the "genre shame" she once felt and, fueled by new ideas and her readers' enthusiasm, continues to revel in writing YA fiction.

hand at adult fiction, Roth responded, "I love my readers so much and I have so many ideas that fit into that young-adult category. I know that's where I want to be, but there's so much freedom to do any genre, especially weird things. It's a great time to be a YA writer now."

ROTH'S RECOMMENDED READS

When it comes to the books and the authors who have influenced her, Veronica has a solid list of notable titles and writers. In interview after interview, she discusses how powerful she found Lois Lowry's *The Giver*. *Brave New World* by Aldous Huxley is another title in the literary canon that Veronica loves. Other books on her list include *1984* by George Orwell, *Ender's Game* by Orson Scott Card, and Frank Herbert's *Dune*. She loves the *Animorphs* series created by K A. Applegate as well as the seven-book story of wizard Harry Potter by J. K. Rowling. She professes to read absolutely anything by Flannery O'Connor, and when she was growing up, she also read Judy Blume.

On her blog (http://veronicarothbooks.blogspot.com/), she offers a list of additional book recommendations, so anyone looking for another Roth-recommended read has plenty from which to choose.

LOVE AND ROMANCE AND SMOOCHING

With two strong characters like Tris and Four, many readers expect a romance, and Roth does not disappoint. She doesn't just throw in some gratuitous sex and kissing, or "smooching" as she likes to call it. She defines romance as an intersection of friendship and attraction, so she tries to make sure that the characters in her book have "actual conversations about things other than their feelings for each other—and to develop their friendship on the page," she said in an interview with Serena Chase of the *USA Today* website.

Roth was able to draw on her own admittedly limited experience (she says she only had two serious relationships, one of which ended in her marriage to photographer Nelson Fitch). She told Chase:

> I think that's how I see love. I see it developing from friendship. Common ground is a strong basis for friendship. My husband is my best friend and we have a lot in common even though we're admittedly different people. I think it evolves from how I see relationships working. You know, the opposites attract thing happens all the time, but so does

Shailene Woodley and Theo James play Tris and Four in the *Divergent* film, bringing the romantic tension from Roth's novels straight to the silver screen.

the best friends thing. It's just a great kind of relationship in fiction.

She wanted to make sure the friendship between Tris and Four felt authentic, so she purposely avoided creating a love triangle, preferring instead to explore the challenges a relationship faces through her trilogy. Roth was careful to make sure that, because hers are action-based books, the romance scenes didn't slow down the book's pace too much and bore her action-loving readers. At the same time, she wanted to be sure to take the time to create the strong connection she wanted between Four and Tris. The romantic tension certainly moved the plot along in its own way.

IN SEARCH OF UTOPIA

To hear her tell it, Roth didn't exactly plan out her stories but, rather, figured out a lot of things along the way. As she wrote, she realized that her supposed utopia was actually quite the opposite: it was a dystopia. Instead of becoming better people, she explained in an interview with Goodreads, the faction members became "narrower, twisted versions of themselves, and they ripped each other apart. It was a really strange experience, to realize that I would be a terrible God. Humbling, definitely."

She explored human nature and came to realize how, even with the best intentions, people can end up doing more harm than good. But on the brighter side, she also discovered that sometimes people can find the strength to be good and do the right thing even when they are in the middle of bedlam. In this latter respect, then, the *Divergent* trilogy is the utopia Roth would have purposely created—one in which everyone was trying, in his or her own way, to be a better person.

THE FIVE FACTIONS IN HER FICTION

Throughout the books, five factions are in play. A character in *Divergent*, Marcus Eaton, explains the reason for the factions:

> Decades ago our ancestors realized that it is not political ideology, religious belief, race, or nationalism that is to blame for a warring world. Rather, they determined that it was the fault of human personality—of humankind's inclination toward evil, in whatever form that is. They divided into factions that sought to eradicate those qualities they believed responsible for the world's disarray.

The first faction Roth came up with was Dauntless; then she wondered what

53

qualities she would choose if it were up to her to make this world. Finally, she came up with her final five: Dauntless (the brave), Amity (the peaceful), Erudite (the intelligent), Candor (the truthful), and Abnegation (the selfless). Along with the five factions, there are also the people who give the series its name: the Divergent.

HIGH SCHOOL: THE ULTIMATE DYSTOPIA

In retrospect, maybe Roth should not be surprised to find that her unintentional dystopia is so popular. Young people who read YA fiction such as hers, including the *Hunger Games* series by Suzanne Collins, might seem preoccupied with what seems like a dismal future because high school can feel

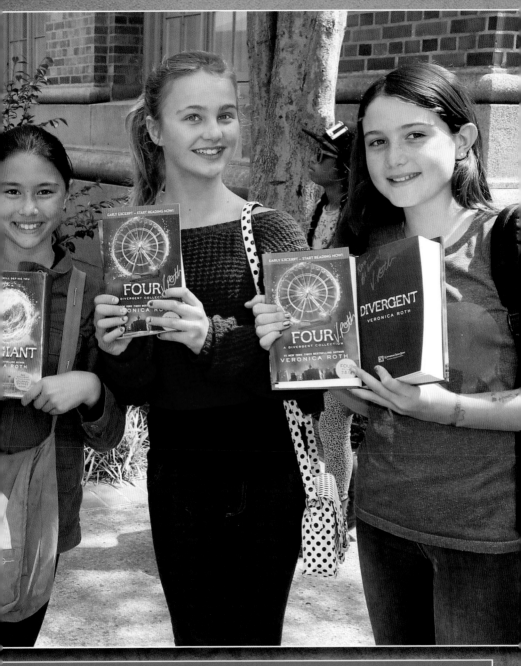

Maybe one reason teens read Roth's dystopian novels with such voracity is because they can relate so well as they try to get through the difficulties of high school.

a lot like that, she says. Roth did not particularly enjoy high school and doesn't know many people who did. During high school, she has said, you start to see that "the world is not as pretty and shiny as it seemed when you were a child. So dystopian and futuristic books seem like a way of acknowledging the difficulties that teenagers are encountering, or at least noticing that they exist."

FIGURING OUT THE FACTIONS

Because she is a big fan of J.K. Rowling's *Harry Potter* books, maybe it's not such a stretch that Roth categorizes the characters who populate her books. Rowling's budding wizards are divided into four dormitories that, like Roth's factions, are also heavily

Divergent's factions echo J. K. Rowling's *Harry Potter* series, in which young wizards are divided into houses by a sorting hat, introduced here by Professor McGonagall, played by Maggie Smith.

based on personality traits. In the *Divergent* books, all sixteen-year-olds must go through a simulated test to determine their aptitudes. Based on their actions under the simulations, such as whether or not to dive in the path of a vicious, attacking dog to save another person's life, their factions are suggested (although they have the option to choose another if they want).

"I have this long-standing fascination with personality tests," Roth admitted in an interview with Janet Potter from the *Chicago Reader*. "I was obsessed with defining myself or fitting myself into a category, and as I grew older I realized how harmful that is. It doesn't allow you to grow. Maybe the book is grappling with that."

Most of the characters opt to remain in the faction in which they grew up, but occasionally, people go against the aptitude results and, for one reason or another, choose another faction. Most people in the book seem to fit neatly into one faction or another. Tris, however, is an exception. Instead of one faction, she shows strengths for three, which is not only unusual, but also dangerous. In Tris's world, she is considered Divergent, a group that leaders deem dangerous because such people can't be controlled. The only thing worse than being a Divergent is being factionless. The factionless people don't belong to any faction at all and live on the outskirts of the society.

THE NAME GAME

Roth is constantly asked by young readers if the names of the various factions were something she conjured up herself. In fact, the names are each real words, deliberately selected by Roth mainly because she thought they would be unfamiliar to many. Her reasoning behind using these names was threefold. First, by choosing more unusual words, she hoped to slow readers down a bit so that they would better understand what each faction represented. Second, she felt that the definitions of the less familiar words were specific and interesting. And finally, as she wrote on her blog, she thought "they sound cooler."

On her blog, Roth offers the definitions for each faction's name. These are Dauntless, Abnegation, Amity, Candor, and Erudite. Some of her "wordy" fans have also noticed that not all the faction names are the same parts of speech. Candor, Amity, and Abnegation are all nouns, whereas Dauntless and Erudite are both adjectives. As she revised the book, she put some thought into whether or not they should all be the same part of speech, but she ultimately decided against it. In the end, she figured that each faction would have decided on its own name, manifesto, customs, and rules without regard to any of the other factions, so it wasn't likely that their names would be that similar.

DAUNTLESS

Dauntless is the first faction Roth conjured up. The word describes one who is courageous in the face of danger or difficulty and who does not get discouraged. The Dauntless blame cowardice for the problems of their world. They don't shy away from a good adrenaline rush, and they never let anyone boss them around. They will do anything—no matter how scary, no matter how tough—if they think it's the right thing. Following their train of thought, if everyone would stop being afraid to do what it takes to make things right, all would be well. Dauntless come off as rough to others, but they are tough and daring, too.

Every faction member can be recognized on sight just by what they are wearing. The Dauntless look and dress as boldly as they act. They wear black and sport tattoos and piercings. Parents and kids alike have every unnatural hair color imaginable.

The Dauntless faction, known by sight by their black clothes, tattoos, and piercings, face their fears and are renowned for their toughness and bravery.

The Dauntless faction came about from Roth's psychology class at Carleton College, in which she studied exposure therapy. In exposure therapy, patients heal by facing their fears. The Dauntless faction members do this all the time and reserve their highest praise for bravery.

ABNEGATION

Abnegation means denial of oneself or giving up something. Members of the selfless Abnegation faction point a finger at selfishness, blaming that trait for their society's problems. The members of this faction eschew attention. Instead, they find joy in helping others be happy, content, safe, and healthy. The Abnegation feel that if people were less selfish, the world would be a much better place. Although it can seem hard to get to know people from this faction, they are reputed to be gentle, peaceful individuals.

Because Abnegation try not to draw attention to themselves, they wear loose clothes in shades of gray. They keep their hairstyles plain, too, all in hopes that they will be less aware of themselves and their appearance and more in tune with others.

AMITY

Amity, which means friendship and harmony, is the faction of peace. Roth refers to it as the faction with the most artists and poets. They love music. If everyone is getting along, the Amity are happy. They love to laugh and seek happiness however they can. Sometimes this makes them come across as silly and uncertain, but the Amity are also known to be relaxed and sincere. They place the blame for war squarely on aggression.

Amity are known on sight because of their warm, bright outfits. The girls tend to wear dresses and skirts, but overall the Amity are not opposed to wearing clothes from other factions. So, as Roth points out on her blog, an Erudite who transferred to the Amity could wear jeans without a problem.

CANDOR

Members of the Candor faction live their lives in an open and honest way. They blame war on duplicity, or deceitfulness. They are honest with everyone, all the time, even when it isn't easy and results in trouble. Because they would always rather hear the truth, they don't take things personally. It's hard to insult them. In their ideal world, everyone would be straightforward and plainspoken. This means they can come across as insensitive, but they are just as apt to be considered honorable and self-assured.

The basic Candor outfit is a bit more on the formal side than the dress of other factions. Men wear a white shirt and black tie to reflect their black-and-white worldview. As Roth describes them in *Divergent*, "Their faction values honesty and sees the truth as black and white, so that is what they wear."

ERUDITE

The word "erudite" means having great knowledge, or being scholarly. Those who choose the Erudite faction love to learn and to figure out how things function. Their decisions are based solely on logic, never a gut feeling and certainly not emotions. They feel that the world would be a much better place if everyone had a proper education and made learning his or her top priority. The Erudite value knowledge over intelligence because they feel that intelligence is something one is born with, whereas knowledge is something one can achieve. Members of this faction can come off as condescending, as if they believe they are smarter or somehow better than everyone else, but they are just as likely to be viewed as smart and perceptive. They tend to think that ignorance was the cause of their society's downfall.

By wearing one item of blue, Roth could have passed for an Erudite when she attended the Summit Entertainment Comic-Con VIP Celebration Red Carpet.

The best description of Erudite fashion is right in the book *Divergent* itself: "Erudite faction norms dictate that a faction member must wear at least one blue article of clothing at a time, because blue causes the body to release calming chemicals, and 'a calm mind is a clear mind.' The color has also come to signify their faction." When Roth herself got gussied up in Erudite style for her blog, she wore a blue button-down shirt and simple blue jeans as she pretended to shush loud talkers in a library.

DIVERGENT

As explained on Roth's blog, to diverge means "to move, lie, or extend in different directions from a common point; branch off." More to the point regarding members of this group in the book, diverge means "to differ in opinion, character, form, etc.; deviate."

The Divergent are a special group. They don't fit neatly into any one faction; rather, they show \an aptitude for belonging to several factions. The Divergent keep this fact about themselves a secret because various faction leaders feel that those with multiple aptitudes cannot be controlled and therefore should be considered dangerous.

A SIXTH FACTION?

In an interview on Amazon, Roth was asked what she would do if she was asked to create one more faction for her *Divergent* world. She explained that when she came up with the five factions, she tried to cover a wide range of different virtues: "Abnegation, for example, includes five of the traditional 'seven heavenly virtues:' chastity, temperance, charity, patience, and humility."

However, if pressed, she would make a sixth faction based on industriousness. The people in this faction would be thorough and hard workers, and idleness would not be tolerated. Members of this faction would always be at work, always moving. Like the other factions, the Industrious would be just as likely to overdo it and take their work too far. Roth wasn't sure what they would wear, but her guess would be overalls.

THE FICTION WRITER'S FACTION

Roth is often asked what faction she would choose if she were part of the *Divergent* society.

Over the short history of her writing career, she has changed her mind a few times. She believes that as a sixteen-year-old, she would have chosen to be part of Candor, those totally truthful people. As a teen, she had some trouble trusting people, and Candor would have felt like a safe place where she'd know where she stood with everyone.

In 2011, she thought perhaps Dauntless would have been her faction of choice because of her own struggle to be brave. "I think bravery makes you selfless, it makes you honest, it makes you trust people. Brave is something I want to be," she explained during a Goodreads interview. Her own anxiety

Once Roth thought her faction would be Dauntless, based on her desire to be brave and "tough," but on further reflection she decided Abnegation would be a better fit.

69

has been known to make her feel trapped, which she feels has kept her from making ideal choices for the people in her life.

Later, Roth decided Abnegation would have been her choice. As she explained to the Collider website's Christina Radish, "I used to think that I would choose dauntless. I think that's a desire that a lot of people have, to be a bad-ass. But, I'm not. So, I think I would actually choose abnegation."

FACTIONS AND FAITH

The factions in Roth's trilogy can be seen as having characteristics influenced by her Christian faith, traits such as courage, meekness, wisdom, peace, and truth. Yet the author does not describe her books as "Christian," per se. As she explained to interviewer Elizabeth Baird-Hardy in 2013, "Tris's story is not 'Christian' any more or less than other stories that feel somehow true to people. I am committed to a particular faith, yes, but my intention is always just to tell the most honest story I can, even when those stories are obviously not 'factual.'"

Roth goes on to explain that she feels each faction does support a particular moral viewpoint, but to the point that the *Divergent* society almost suffocates its people as it forces them to behave a certain way. She sees this as a common problem in Christian culture, too, as the devout frequently focus on a behavior they think is "right" and judge others who don't live up to those expectations. The trouble with that, she says, is that:

> ...by paring everything down to those elements, we lose what makes our faith alive and active and beautiful and humbling, which is the love and acceptance of God despite all our inevitable and constant failure to be perfect. Striving for moral perfection, the way the factions do, is just another way of trying to prove your worth when that's just suffocating and pointless—you don't have to prove your worth. You are already worthy; you're worthy and broken, all at the same time.

CHAPTER FIVE

CHARACTERS FROM PAGE TO SCREEN

J ust as she carefully chose the name of each faction, Veronica Roth took great pains with the names of her characters. Her high school English teacher, June Kramer, says that even as a teenager, Roth was intensely aware of the people and the world around her. "She's a student of human behavior. She's got this acute sensitivity and awareness," adds Kramer. "She takes delight in little things. She notices details and lets them please her. She's very aware. You can imagine her dystopian world because she makes it come alive with real things and real people."

Roth cheerfully signs autographs and chats with fans at an *Ender's Game* and *Divergent* cast autograph signing at Comic-Con International.

THE NAME-CHANGE GAME

Veronica's fascination with names goes back to her childhood. First, her mother sometimes called her Nikki, a nickname short for Veronica, and then other people wanted to call her Ronnie. She flatly refused to respond to either name. Eventually, she chose her own nickname: V, which she liked because, as she put it in *The World of Divergent*, it wasn't "cutesy or girly." The other names just didn't fit her personality.

Names have strength, and changing them can cause someone to create an entirely new identity. Veronica also feels that, from a religious angle, name changing can be very significant. In the Jewish faith, after a person in the Torah faces God, he or she is given a new name: Abram becomes Abraham, Sarai becomes Sarah. People in the Christian Bible change their names after encountering God as well; Saul is forever known as Paul after his conversion. A name change such as this typically signifies that a transformation either is about to or already has taken place. Such changes are evident in more recent books and movies, too. Mr. Anderson becoming Neo in the *Matrix* movies, Anakin Skywalker morphing into Darth Vader in the *Star Wars* saga, Andrew Wiggin becoming Ender in *Ender's Game* and its sequels, and Tom Riddle turning into Voldemort in the *Harry Potter* books are some examples that Roth cites.

The name game makes an appearance in Roth's books as well. Tobias undergoes such a significant change that he feels his name no longer fits him. He comes to view Tobias as a scared boy and instead chooses to be known as Four, who, in his mind, is a strong adult, trying to put aside the pain of his past. Eventually, he realizes he can't totally escape who he used to be, especially when the past keeps coming up in his personal fear simulation, which all the Dauntless must endure. When he meets Tris and realizes she is someone he can trust, he tells her his real name.

Tris also changes her name the day she chooses to join the Dauntless. In the beginning, as a member of Abnegation, she goes by Beatrice, but when she changes factions, she knows she needs a new start. Deciding that Beatrice "doesn't sound right any-more," she confidently renames herself Tris.

PUTTING THINGS IN PLACE

Initially, as Roth furiously keyed out her first draft, she didn't have any particular location in mind. The more she wrote, however, and as she revised, the more strongly she felt that the story would be stronger and more realistic if it unfolded in a specific place. The more she looked at her work, the more she realized she'd almost already done just that. Throughout the book, there were traits of present-day Chicago in the Divergent dystopia. The incessantly moving, elevated trains—a future version of the city's famous "L" (slang for "elevated")—probably had the strongest influence on Roth in terms of putting the story in place. She describes them as practically being a creature: con-stantly moving but with no obvious driver.

Once she had the place in position, Roth needed to decide where the factions would be

As Roth wrote *Divergent*, she subconsciously set it in her beloved Chicago, shown here in a still from the film, which was also set in the city.

located. She opted to put Abnegation in Chicago's North Side, where there are a lot of neighborhood-heavy areas. Although Dauntless couldn't possibly be located in a real place—she describes it as having underground areas and underground rivers—she envisions it as farther south. She placed Candor in Merchandise Mart, which is her favorite building in the city. A line of buildings directly across from the Art Institute struck her as the perfect setting for Erudite. Finally, she needed a place for Amity, but she couldn't pin down a place within the city that fit them just right, so she fabricated that out of her imagination.

FACTIONS ON FILM

Maybe it was a bit serendipitous that Veronica set her books in Chicago, because that very city turned out to be the perfect place to produce the *Divergent* movie, which was released in 2014. Summit Entertainment had bought the rights several months before the book even hit the shelves. In fact, Roth had a book deal for the trilogy at this point but hadn't even written *Insurgent* or *Allegiant*. By October 2012, direc-

tor Neil Burger had agreed to direct the film. He is known for his films *The Illusionist* and *Limitless*,

Director Neil Burger, on the left with stars from the *Divergent* movie in the center and Roth at right, put the nervous author at ease once they talked and she realized how well he knew her book.

both of which Roth described on her blog as being "dynamic and interesting."

Even though Roth admired Burger's movies, she had some misgivings. She was nervous about putting her work into someone else's hands. What author wouldn't have some trepidation about handing over her carefully crafted story? And this being her first time working with a movie crew adapting her work, she just didn't know what to expect. After talking to Burger on the phone, however, she felt reassured. She realized he was well acquainted with her books, and he asked very good questions. She admitted on her blog, "I actually found myself wishing he had been around while I was writing, to help me think through the particularities of the world of *Divergent*!"

JUMPING TO THE SILVER SCREEN

Roth might seem like an ideal fit to write the screenplay for the movie adaptation of her own novel, but when it came down to it, she didn't want much to do with the screenwriting. Part of her reluctance had to do with her ideas about the setting, which seemed a bit misty. "It's like squinting at something from afar," she told Christina Radish of the Collider website.

CAN SHE CAMEO?

As the days led up to the release of the *Divergent* film, speculation was high. One question was whether or not the author would have a cameo in the movie. The Page to Premiere website speculated that she would play one of the top power players in Dauntless or another minor background character.

If Roth were offered a cameo in the film, she would jump at the chance. Given the choice, she'd like to play one of the Dauntless initiates trying to jump on or off the train—although, as she told Brooke Tarnoff of the Next Movie website, "I don't think they'd let me do that, because I'm uncoordinated and have poor balance." Still, she thinks it would be fun to play a part in a movie based on her books.

When all is said and done, Roth acknowledges that she is not a filmmaker, but a writer.

Instead, the honor of writing the *Divergent* screenplay went to screenwriter Evan Daugherty, whose credits include *Snow White and the Huntsman*. "Simplicity is easy to come by," said Daugherty. "But a simple thing done well is hard to

Evan Daugherty, already known for his work on the movie *Snow White and the Huntsman*, wrote the *Divergent* screenplay.

beat. Veronica nailed a very primal, relatable idea: You turn 16 and you choose what you think is going to be some narrow version of how the rest of your life is going to look."

Roth had not read a draft of the script before production of the movie began, but she appreciated how closely Daugherty's screenplay seemed to stick to the book. She admits that the movie isn't exactly how she pictured it, but, as she told Radish, "I would be a little disappointed, if it were exactly how I'd pictured it, because then there's no reinterpretation and no new discovery." She was very particular, however, when it came to the casting. Roth felt it was important to find actors who could play the character's personality, which was far more critical to her than having their appearance match the way she described the characters in the book. In a couple of cases, she wasn't sure the filmmakers had chosen the right actors for the parts, but once she saw them act, she was convinced that they had done well with the casting.

Although she was more of an observer than an active participant in the filming process, she decided she should go to the set. The success of the film would reflect back on her, after all, regardless of how much she had to do with it. She even had a director's chair on the set of *Divergent*. She

Shailene Woodley, Veronica Roth, and Neil Burger *(left to right)* got a chance to visit on the movie set during filming.

told Christopher Borrelli of the *Chicago Tribune* that when she walked on to the set for the first time, she thought, "It's like walking into my brain."

EPILOGUE

As a YA writer who was first published in only her early twenties, Roth has already had huge successes, with more likely to come. After finishing the *Divergent* series, she decided to take a break from writing for a while. She told Janet Potter that she has spent so much of her life writing that she never found the time to develop many outside interests. So as for her immediate plans for her writing downtime, she told Potter, "Maybe I'll get hobbies."

FACT SHEET

ON VERONICA ROTH

Birth date: August 19, 1988

Birthplace: New York

Current residence: Near Chicago, IL

First publication: *Divergent*; debuted on the *New York Times* best-seller list

Age when first book was published: 22

Marital status: Married to photographer Nelson Fitch

Colleges attended: Carleton College and Northwestern University

Height: Six feet tall (183 cm)

Writing motto: "One thing at a time"

Preferred writing font: Times New Roman

Divergent playlist: 99 percent Florence and the Machine

Authors who inspired her to start writing: Lois Lowry, Sharon Creech, Jerry Spinelli, Diana Wynne Jones, Frank Herbert

Career if she wasn't a writer: Editor

Hobbies: Cooking

Interests: Psychology, biology, theology (John Calvin and Augustine), fashion, contemporary art, and poetry (Edna St. Vincent Millay)

Favorite sport team: Chicago Bears

Recurrent dream: About bugs; she doesn't know why

ON VERONICA ROTH'S WORK

NOVELS

Divergent. HarperCollins, April 25, 2011

Synopsis: In dystopian Chicago, society is divided into five factions: Candor, Abnegation, Dauntless, Amity, and Erudite. On a certain day every year, all sixteen-year-olds must select which faction they will be for the rest of their lives. Beatrice must decide between staying with her family or choosing the faction she feels she truly is. Her choice surprises everyone, including herself. Renaming herself Tris, she goes through initiation, struggling to find her place in the world and who her true friends are. She also finds herself in a relationship with a boy, Four, who both fascinates and irritates her. But Tris also has a secret, one that could destroy her. As her seemingly perfect world threatens to fall apart, she comes to realize that her secret might actually save her and those she loves.

FACT SHEET

Insurgent. HarperCollins, May 1, 2012

Synopsis: Choices have consequences, as Tris Prior
comes to discover in the course of the story.
Tris's initiation day, which should have been a
celebration, has turned into a horrific nightmare,
leaving her full of guilt and grief. Chicago's factions are now on the brink of war. Choices must
be made, including which side to take in the
conflict, and decisions will take on more weight
than ever before. Aware that her secret could be
revealed at any time, Tris navigates the tricky ter-
rain of shifting allegiances among the factions as
she comes to the conclusion that she must ultimately be true to herself and fully embrace her
Divergence.

Allegiant. HarperCollins, October 22, 2013

Synopsis: Order in faction-based, dystopian
Chicago has been upended due to violence,
power struggles, loss, and betrayal. Tris seeks
the escape of exploring the world past the lim-
its she's known, believing that perhaps beyond
the fence, she and Tobias will find a simple
new life together. But her new life turns out
to be anything but simple. The truth puts her
happiness in peril once again. In *Allegiant*, Tris
faces a whole new set of impossible choices
about courage, allegiance, sacrifice, and love.

SHORT STORIES

Roth has published a number of short stories in
novella form, including:

Free Four. HarperCollins, August 7, 2012

Synopsis: This story is basically a retelling of an
important scene in *Divergent*, told from a new
point of view. Readers get a first-person take on
the character Tobias ("Four"), who shares previously unknown facts and fascinating details
about himself, his past, his own initiation, and
his thoughts about Tris.

Four: A Divergent Collection. HarperCollins,
July 8, 2014

Synopsis: This compilation of short stories also
is told from the perspective of Tobias. In these
tales, readers witness Tobias's aptitude test,
Choosing Day, and the moment he is given his
new name. The four stories in the collection are
(in alphabetic order) "The Initiate," "The Son,"
"The Traitor," and "The Transfer."

CONTRIBUTING WRITER

Must-Read Teen Novel Sampler. New York:
HarperCollins Children's Books, May 8, 2012.

Pitch Dark: Dark Days of Summer Sampler. New York:
HarperCollins Children's Books, April 24, 2012.

Shards and Ashes. New York: HarperCollins Children's Books, February 19, 2013.

OTHER

The World of Divergent: The Path to Allegiant. HarperCollins, July 8, 2014

Synopsis: This bonus book, previously only available in the *Divergent* series box set, includes faction manifestos, a faction quiz, a Q&A with Roth, book playlists, discussion questions, series inspirations, and more.

veronicarothbooks.blogspot.com

Roth started this blog in October 2011. In it she answers frequently asked questions and shares her thoughts on many subjects. Roth also contributes to the YA Highway blog (www.yahighway.com).

AWARDS

National Council of Teachers of English Award in Writing

The 2014 21st Century Award, from the Chicago Public Library Foundation and the Chicago Public Library.

Divergent

Goodreads Favorite Book of 2011

Goodreads Best Young Adult Fantasy & Science Fiction

New York Times Best Seller

Black-Eyed Susan Book Award winner 2012–2013

Booklist 2012 Best Fiction for Young Adults

Booklist 2012 Quick Pick for Reluctant Young
Adult Readers

Number one in Young Adult Library Services
Association (YALSA) 2012 Teens' Top Ten

Insurgent

Children's Teen Choice Book Award Finalist: 2013

New York Times Best Seller

Best Goodreads Author 2012

2013 Book Week Teen Book of the Year Nominee

Allegiant

New York Times Best Seller

2014 Teen Book of the Year from the Children's
Book Council

Divergent

"A memorable, unpredictable journey from which it
is nearly impossible to turn away." —*Publishers
Weekly* (starred review)

"You'll be up all night with *Divergent*, a brainy thrill-
ride of a novel." —*BookPage*

"*Divergent* holds its own in the genre, with brisk
pacing, lavish flights of imagination and writing that occasionally startles with fine detail …
Divergent clearly has thrills, but it also movingly
explores a more common adolescent anxiety—
the painful realization that coming into one's
own sometimes means leaving family behind,
both ideologically and physically." —Susan
Dominus, *New York Times*

"I found the concept of being persecuted for your
identity fascinating in this book, as it's especially
pertinent to us in our current society." —*The
Guardian*

"A taut and shiveringly exciting read! Tris is
exactly the sort of unflinching and fierce
heroine I love. I couldn't turn the pages
fast enough." —Melissa Marr, *New York*

Times best-selling author of the Wicked
Lovely series

"*Divergent* is a captivating, fascinating book that
kept me in constant suspense and was never
short on surprises. It will be a long time before
I quit thinking about this haunting vision of the
future."—James Dashner, *New York Times* best-
selling author of *The Maze Runner*

Insurgent

"The next big thing."—*Rolling Stone*

"Roth knows how to write. The novel's love story,
intricate plot, and unforgettable setting work in
concert to deliver a novel that will rivet fans of
the first book."—*Publishers Weekly*

"*Insurgent* explores several critical themes, including
the importance of family and the crippling power
of grief at its loss. A very good read."—*School
Library Journal*

"The depth and richness of Beatrice herself make
this an accessible option for both sci-fi buffs and
realistic fiction fans."—Bulletin of the Center for
Children's Books

Allegiant

"A surprise ending that is gutsier and much less predictable than the rest of the series would lead one to expect."—*Los Angeles Times*

"Roth's plotting is...intelligent and complex. Dangers, suspicion, and tension lurk around every corner, and the chemistry between Tris and Tobias remains heart-poundingly real. This final installment will capture and hold attention until the divisive final battle has been waged."—*Publishers Weekly*

"The tragic conclusion, although shocking, is thematically consistent; the bittersweet epilogue offers a poignant hope."—*Kirkus Reviews*

"In this powerful follow-up to the smash hit *Divergent*, feisty orphan Tris threads her way through a dystopian world in which warring factions vie for dominance. Earns apt comparisons with *The Hunger Games*, but this is no imitation."—Barnes & Noble

"In the end, this is a world replete with loss, and the heroes must suffer their own in a twist that will break the hearts of many readers but stays true to the merciless dystopia that Roth has created."—Bulletin of the Center for Children's Books

1988 Veronica is born on August 19.

2006 Veronica graduates from Barrington High School.

2007 Roth transfers from Carleton College to Northwestern University. She is drawn to Northwestern's creative writing program.

2010 In March, Roth meets her agent, Joanna Stampfel-Volpe, at a writer's conference. That April, just one month later, she sells her book to a publisher.

Roth graduates from Northwestern University with a Bachelor of Arts degree on May 7.

2011 Roth marries Nelson Fitch.

Divergent is published. It is voted Goodreads Favorite Book, Goodreads Best Young Adult Fantasy & Science Fiction, one of *Publisher's Weekly* Best 20 Books of 2011, and one of the Amazon Best Books of 2011: Young Adult.

2012 *Insurgent* is published and voted the top Young Adult Fantasy & Science Fiction book for 2012 on the Goodreads website.

Roth is voted Best Goodreads Author.

2013 *Allegiant* is published on October 22 and breaks first-day records for publisher HarperCollins with 455,000 copies sold. It is number one on *USA Today*'s Best-Selling Books list and voted the Best Young Adult Fantasy & Science Fiction book for 2013 on the Goodreads website.

Divergent wins Black-Eyed Susan Book Award for 2012–2013

2014 *Divergent* wins the Evergreen Young Adult Book Award for 2014, the 2014 California Young Reader Medal in the Young Adult category, and the Grand Canyon Reader Award: Teen.

A film based on the first book in the *Divergent* series is released on March 21.

Summit Entertainment announces that the second movie, *Insurgent*, will be released in 2015.

ABNEGATION The act of refusing or renouncing something.

ALLEGIANT Loyal or committed.

ALTRUISTIC Exhibiting a selfless concern for others.

AMITY Friendship or a feeling of harmony and peace.

APTITUDE An innate ability or talent.

BEDLAM A place or state of chaos or confusion.

CAMEO A small character or part in a movie, usually played by a celebrity.

CANDOR The characteristic of being sincere or honest.

DAUNTLESS Exhibiting bravery or fearlessness.

DIVERGENT Diverging, or being different.

DUPLICITY Deceitfully hiding one's intentions.

DYSTOPIA A fictional place where life is dreadful, verging on terrifying.

ERUDITE Exhibiting knowledge or impressive learning.

ESCHEW To avoid on purpose.

GENRE A distinct form of literature (or music or art) marked by a particular style or content.

INDUSTRIOUSNESS The ability to keep busy or work hard.

INITIATE Someone who is being introduced into an organization.

INSURGENT Someone who rebels against leaders or authority.

MANIFESTO A group's or person's public written statement of policies, aims, and opinions.

GLOSSARY

PITCH To present or promote, or to make a bid, often in a high-pressure way.

PROTAGONIST The main character.

PSYCHOTHERAPY The treatment of a mental illness by psychology rather than medicine.

SCIENCE FICTION A type of fiction about future people or societies and how they are affected by fictional developments in science.

SIMULATION An imitation or model of something.

SPECULATIVE FICTION A type of fiction that includes science fiction, horror, and fantasy.

TRILOGY A collection of three connected novels, plays, films, operas, or albums.

UTOPIA An imaginary place where everything is perfect.

VIRTUE Conduct exhibiting high ethical values.

Anxiety and Depression Association of America (ADAA)
8701 Georgia Avenue #412
Silver Spring, MD 20910
(240) 485-1001
Website: http://www.adaa.org
ADAA strives to use education, practice, and
    research to prevent, treat, and cure disorders
    related to anxiety, depression, and stress.

Anxiety Disorders Association of Canada
101-631 Columbia St.
New Westminster, BC V3M 1A7
Canada
(888) 223-2252
Website: http://www.anxietycanada.ca/english
This Canadian group aims to promote a better under-
    standing about anxiety disorders and offer support
    to people who suffer from them.

British Columbia Science Fiction Association (BCFA)
c/o 209-3851 Francis Road
Richmond, BC V7C 1J6
Canada
Website: http://www.bcsfa.net
BCFA is a general science fiction club covering
    "anything at all to do with SF that you can think
    of—and finally, the phenomenon of SF fandom in
    and of itself."

Freedom From Fear
308 Seaview Avenue
Staten Island, NY 10305
(718) 351-1717 ext. 19
Website: http://www.freedomfromfear.org
Freedom From Fear is a national not-for-profit mental
    health advocacy association founded in 1984 by
    Mary Guardino.

The Hugo Awards
World Science Fiction Society
PO Box 426159
Kendall Square Station
Cambridge, MA 02142
Email: info@thehugoawards.org
Website: http://www.thehugoawards.org
The Hugo Award, science fiction's most celebrated
    award, has been presented every year since 1955.

The Merchandise Mart
222 W Merchandise Mart Plaza
Chicago, IL 60654
(800) 677-6278
Website: http://www.mmart.com
This huge building is home to many wholesale design
    shops and also has shops open to the general
    public. It opened in 1930 and is one of Chicago's
    signature buildings. It is also one of Veronica Roth's
    favorite buildings.

New England Science Fiction Association, Inc. (NESFA)
PO Box 809
Framingham, MA 01701
(617) 625-2311
Email: info@nesfa.org
Website: http://www.nesfa.org
Founded in 1967, the New England Science Fiction
Association, Inc. (NESFA) is among the oldest New
England science fiction clubs. It focuses on its
annual convention, Boskone, and NESFA Press.

Science Fiction and Fantasy Writers of America (SFWA)
PO Box 3238
Enfield, CT 06083
Website: http://www.sfwa.org
The SWFA is an organization that supports, endorses,
advocates, and defends writers of science fiction,
fantasy, and related genres. It hosts the celebrated
Nebula Awards.

SF Canada
7433 East River Road
Washago, ON L0K 2B0
Canada
Website: http://northbynotwest.com/sfcanada-wp
Originally named Canada's National Association for
Speculative Fiction Professionals in 1989, in 1992
it was incorporated as SF Canada. The main goal
of SF Canada is to encourage a community among

members of the speculative fiction community, which includes writers of "science fiction, fantasy, horror and any other weird fiction that invokes a sense of wonder."

Washington Science Fiction Association (WSFA)
c/o Sam Lubell
11801 Rockville Pike #1508
Rockville, MD 20852
Website: http://wsfa.org
The WSFA is Washington D.C.'s oldest science fiction organization. Members include those who are interested in all kinds of science fiction and fantasy, including "fantasy and science fiction films, television, costuming, gaming, filming, convention-running, etc."

WEBSITES

Because of the changing nature of Internet links, Rosen Publishing has developed an online list of websites related to the subject of this book. This site is updated regularly. Please use the following link to access the list:

http://www.rosenlinks.com/AAA/Roth

Anderson, Laurie Halse. *Speak*. New York, NY: Farrar, Straus and Giroux, 1999.

Applegate, Katherine. *The Invasion*. New York, NY: Scholastic Paperbacks, 2011.

Bourne, Edmund J. *The Anxiety & Phobia Workbook*. 5th ed. Oakland, CA: New Harbinger Publications, 2005.

Bova, Ben. *The Craft of Writing Science Fiction that Sells*. N.p.: ReAnimus Press, 2011.

Card, Orson Scott. *Ender's Game*. New York, NY: Tor, 1994.

Claeys, Gregory, ed. *The Cambridge Companion to Utopian Literature*. Cambridge, England: Cambridge University Press, 2010.

Collard, Patrizia. *Mindfulness-Based Cognitive Therapy for Dummies*. Chinchester, England: John Wiley and Sons, 2013.

Dunn, Mary R. *I Want to Write Books* (Dream Jobs). New York, NY: Rosen Publishing, 2009.

Elish, Dan. *The Craft of Writing: Fiction*. New York, NY: Marshall Cavendish Benchmark, 2011.

Hintz, Carrie, and Elaine Ostry, eds. *Utopian and Dystopian Writing for Children and Young Adults*. New York, NY: Routledge, 2009.

James, Edward, and Farah Mendlesohn, eds. *The Cambridge Companion to Science Fiction*. Cambridge, England: Cambridge University Press, 2013.

Knost, Michael, ed. *Writers Workshop of Science Fiction & Fantasy.* Lexington, KY: Seventh Star Press, 2013.

LaMotte, Anne. *Bird by Bird: Some Instructions on Writing and Life.* New York, NY: Anchor, 2007.

L'Engle, Madeleine. *A Wrinkle in Time.* New York, NY: Square Fish, 2007.

Lowry, Lois. *The Giver.* New York, NY: Laurel Leaf, 2002.

Orwell, George. *1984.* New York, NY: Houghton Mifflin, 2013.

Spencer, Anne. *I Get Panic Attacks. Now What?* (Teen Life 411). New York, NY: Rosen Publishing, 2012.

Tompkins, Michael A., and Katherine Martinez. *My Anxious Mind: A Teen's Guide to Managing Anxiety and Panic.* Washington, DC: Magination Press, 2009.

Wehrenbert, Margaret. *The 10 Best-Ever Anxiety Management Techniques: Understanding How Your Brain Makes You Anxious and What You Can Do to Change It.* New York, NY: W. W. Norton & Company, 2008.

Zusak, Markus. *The Book Thief.* New York, NY: Alfred A. Knopf, 2013.

Amazon.com. "A Q&A with Author Veronica Roth."
Retrieved January 25, 2014 (http://www.amazon
.com/Divergent-Trilogy-Veronica-Roth/dp/0062024
027/ref=sr_1_1?s=books&ie=UTF8&qid=13029815
01&sr=1-1).

Baird-Hardy, Elizabeth. "'10 Questions' with Veronica
Roth, author of the Divergent Trilogy: Part 2—
Elizabeth Baird-Hardy's Questions." Hogwarts
Professor: Thoughts for Serious Readers, March 5,
2013. Retrieved June 21, 2014 (http://www
.hogwartsprofessor.com/10-questions-with
-veronica-roth-author-of-the-divergent-trilogy
-part-2-elizabeth-baird-hardys-questions).

Borrelli, Christopher. "Veronica Roth the next literary
superstar?" *Chicago Tribune*, October 21, 2013.
Retrieved December 11, 2013 (http://articles
.chicagotribune.com/2013-10-21/entertainment/
chi-veronica-roth-profile-20131021_1_veronica
-roth-allegiant-anderson).

Chase, Serena. "Interview: Veronica Roth, author
of 'Insurgent.'" USAToday.com, June 19, 2012.
Retrieved February 1, 2014 (http://books.usatoday
.com/happyeverafter/post/2012-06-18/veronica-
roth-interview-insurgent/718819/1).

Codinha, Cotton. "The New Roth." *Elle*, August 20,
2013. Retrieved January 14, 2014 (http://www
.elle.com/pop-culture/best/divergent-author
-veronica-roth-interview).

Constable, Burt. "Barrington English teacher recalls 'Divergent' author." *Daily Herald*, October 22, 2013. Retrieved January 12, 2014 (http://www.dailyherald .com/article/20131022/news/710229937).

Goodreads.com. "Interview with Veronica Roth." December 2011. Retrieved December 28, 2013 (https://www.goodreads.com/interviews/show/637 .Veronica_Roth).

Goodreads.com. "Quotes About Tris." Retrieved January 29, 2014 (https://www.goodreads.com/ quotes/tag/tris).

Harper Teen. "Veronica Roth Q&A." Retrieved January 29, 2014 (http://www.youtube.com/ watch?feature=player_embedded&v=UIYgiR2zD-s).

Kidd, James. "Veronica Roth: Out of the Dark." *Sydney Morning Herald*, January 25, 2014. Retrieved January 25, 2014 (http://www.smh.com.au/ entertainment/books/veronica-roth-out-of-the -dark-20140123-319p8.html).

Potter, Janet. "Veronica Roth Divides to Conquer." *Chicago Reader*, October 22, 2013. Retrieved January 25, 2014 (http://www.chicagoreader.com/ chicago/veronica-roth-divergent-series-allegiant -ya-dystopia/Content?oid=11293593).

Radish, Christina. "Author Veronica Roth Talks DIVERGENT, the Film's Casting, How Neil Burger's Vision Compares to Her Own, the Final Book ALLEGIANT, and More." *Collider*, May 9, 2013.

Retrieved January 17, 2014 (http://collider.com/veronica-roth-divergent-movie-interview).

Roth, Veronica. The Art of Not Writing. Retrieved January 29, 2014 (http://theartofnotwriting.tumblr.com).

Roth, Veronica. *Divergent*. New York, NY: Harper Collins, 2011.

Roth, Veronica. "The First 100 Pages, and the DIVERGENT Dictionary." Veronica Roth Books, April 4, 2011. Retrieved January 26, 2014 (http://veronicarothbooks.blogspot.com/2011/04/first-100-pages-and-divergent.html).

Roth, Veronica. "Recommendation List." Veronica Roth Books, September 23, 2011. Retrieved February 1, 2014 (http://veronicarothbooks.blogspot.com/2011/09/recommendation-list.html).

Roth, Veronica. *The World of Divergent: The Path to Allegiant.* New York, NY: HarperCollins, 2013.

Tarnoff, Brooke. "5 Questions With 'Divergent' Writer Veronica Roth." Next Movie, November 29, 2011. Retrieved January 29, 2014 (http://www.nextmovie.com/blog/divergent-movie-veronica-roth/).

Young, Robin. "'Allegiant' Could Shock Fans of Best-Selling 'Divergent' Books." *Here and Now,* WBUR.org, October 22, 2013. Retrieved January 25, 2014 (http://hereandnow.wbur.org/2013/10/22/allegiant-could-shock).

INDEX

ABOUT THE AUTHOR

Heather Moore Niver is a New York State writer, editor, and voracious reader. She has written more than twenty nonfiction books for children, including *Thrill Seekers: Skydivers*, *20 Fun Facts About Stickbugs*, *Tributaries of the Chesapeake*, and *Wild Wheels: Camaros*.

PHOTO CREDITS

Cover, p. 3 Jeffrey Mayer/WireImage/Getty Images; pp. 6–7 © AP Images; p. 12 KRT/Newscom; pp. 16–17 Eugene Moerman/Shut-tersock.com; p. 21 Ethan Miller/Getty Images; p. 23 Taylor Hill/Getty Images; p. 26 Karwai Tang/Getty Images; p. 29 Araya Diaz/WireImage/Getty Images; pp. 32–33, 84–85 Summit Entertainment/Jaap Buitendijk/AP Images; pp. 36–37 Gerardo Mora/Getty Images; pp. 40–41, 50–51, 60–61, 76–77 Jaap Buitendijk/©Summit Entertainment/courtesy Everett Collection; p. 43 Hulton Archive/Archive Photos/Getty Images; pp. 46–47 Frazer Harrison/Getty Images; pp. 54–55 David Livingston/Getty Images; pp. 56–57 Mary Evans/Warner Bros/JK Rowling/Ronald Grant/Everett Collection (10318454); p. 65, 73 Joe Scarnici/Getty Images; pp. 68–69 Axelle/Bauer-Griffin/FilmMagic/Getty Images; pp. 78–79 Dave M. Benett/WireImage/Getty Images; p. 82 Gregg DeGuire/WireImage/Getty Images; cover, interior pages (book) © www.istockphoto.com/Andrzej Tokarski; cover, interior pages (textured background) javarman/Shutterstock.com; interior pages (clouds) Mihai Simonia/Shutterstock.com.

Designer: Nicole Russo; Editor: Jeanne Nagle; Photo Researcher: Karen Huang